AMAZING ART FORMS

The Art of Dance

BY K. A. HALE

Kids Core
An Imprint of Abdo Publishing
abdobooks.com

abdobooks.com

Published by Abdo Publishing, a division of ABDO, PO Box 398166, Minneapolis, Minnesota 55439.

Printed in the United States of America, North Mankato, Minnesota.
102024
012025

THIS BOOK CONTAINS RECYCLED MATERIALS

Cover Photos: Alen Kadr/Shutterstock Images (tap shoes); Shutterstock Images (ballet shoes); Atif Mahmud/Shutterstock Images (background)
Interior Photos: Dmitry Morgan/Shutterstock Images, 4–5; Shutterstock Images, 6, 7, 28 (left); Chris Ware/Keystone Features/Hulton Archive/Getty Images, 9; TPG/Getty Images News/Getty Images, 10; Anton Vierietin/Shutterstock Images, 12–13; Ian Gavan/Getty Images Entertainment/Getty Images, 15; Hulton Archive/Archive Photos/Getty Images, 16; Alexi Rosenfeld/Getty Images Entertainment/Getty Images, 19; Hiroyuki Ito/Hulton Archive/Getty Images, 20–21; FOX Image Collection/Getty Images, 22; Bettmann/Getty Images, 23; Jana Call Me J./Abaca Press/Alamy Live News/Alamy, 25; Gareth Cattermole/TAS24/Getty Images for TAS Rights Management/Getty Images Entertainment/Getty Images, 26; Sundraw Photography/Shutterstock Images, 28 (right); iStockphoto, 29 (top left), 29 (right), 29 (bottom left)

Editor: Haley Williams
Series Designer: Katharine Hale

Library of Congress Control Number: 2024938357

Publisher's Cataloging-in-Publication Data

Names: Hale, K. A., author.
Title: The art of dance / by K. A. Hale
Description: Minneapolis, Minnesota: ABDO Publishing, 2025 | Series: Amazing art forms | Includes online resources and index.
Identifiers: ISBN 9781098295752 (lib. bdg.) | ISBN 9798384916758 (ebook)
Subjects: LCSH: Art--Juvenile literature. | Dance--Juvenile literature. | Dancers--Juvenile literature. | Dancers in art--Juvenile literature. | Dance and society--Juvenile literature. | Art--Technique--Juvenile literature. | Arts and history--Juvenile literature.
Classification: DDC 793.3--dc23

CONTENTS

There are two styles of ballroom dance. Smooth or standard dances include the waltz, tango, foxtrot, and quickstep. Rhythm or Latin dances include the cha-cha, rumba, samba, and swing.

CHAPTER 1

Ballroom Blitz!

Dev and Prisha walked onto the dance floor with the other pairs of dancers. They were competing in their first ballroom dance competition. They would be competing in six different ballroom dances. The waltz was the first dance of the day.

Older competitive dancers can wear high, thin heels and fancy costumes. Kids have stricter rules. Their clothing must be simpler.

Dev and Prisha were both nervous to compete. But they were also excited.

Dev and Prisha's parents had helped them get ready that morning. Prisha's dad helped her put her hair in a bun. Dev's mom pinned a number to the back of his shirt. The number identified the pair. If the judges liked Dev and Prisha's performance, they would write down the number. Then they would move on in the competition!

How to Waltz

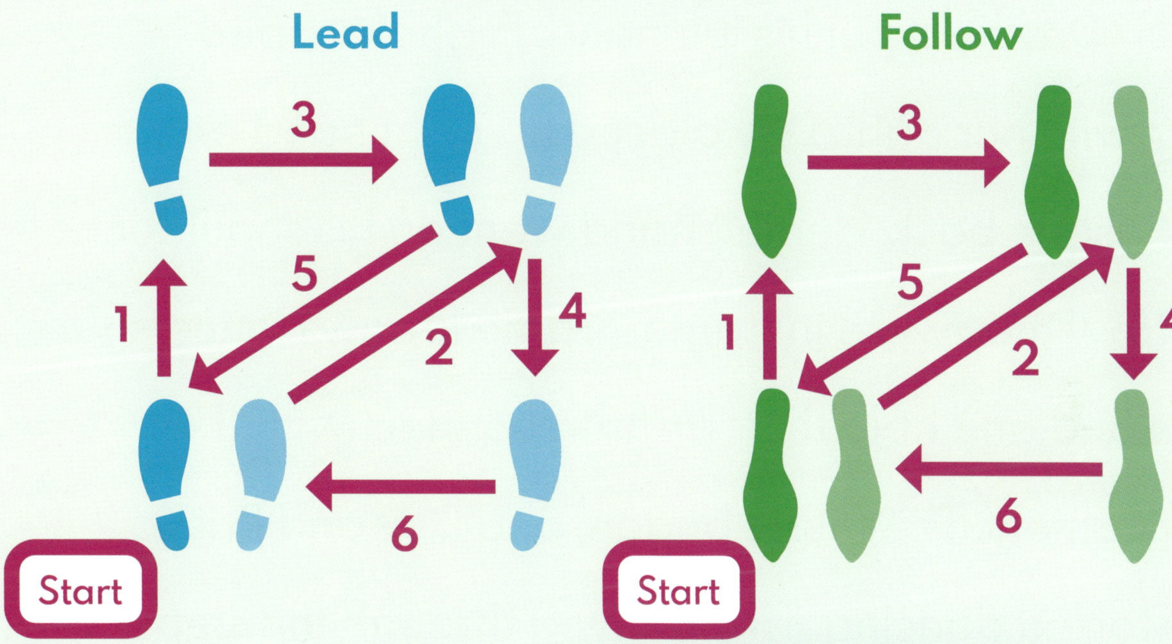

The basic step of the waltz is called the box step. Dancers move in groups of three steps.

Dev was the lead dancer. He would choose what steps to do and when. Prisha was the follow. She would follow Dev's lead. Dev picked out a place on the dance floor. Prisha's skirt swished as she spun into position. They both wore shoes with wide, low heels.

Dev held out his left hand. Prisha clasped it with her right. Dev placed his right hand on Prisha's back. Her left hand went on his shoulder. Now they were in frame. Frame is how dancers stand and hold their arms to connect with their partners. The music began, and Dev and Prisha started dancing. They moved through the steps together. When the music stopped, both dancers

Dance through History

People have danced since **prehistoric** times. Ancient cultures in India, Egypt, China, and Greece showed images of dance in their art. Over time, European social dances evolved into modern ballroom dancing. Many dances have changed over time. But some are the same as when they were first done.

The first ballroom dance competitions were held in Europe in the early 1900s. Ballroom competitions grew around the world starting in the mid-1900s.

took a bow. The audience cheered. Now they would wait and see if they would move on to the next round.

What Is Dance?

Dance is rhythmic movement of the body, often to music. Dance is an art form. It can also be a sport. People dance for many reasons.

People around the world participate in Para dance sport. Wheelchair users can dance alone, with standing partners, or with other wheelchair users.

They may do it to express emotion. Some people dance to tell a story. Others dance for religious reasons or to connect to a culture.

There are hundreds of dance styles. Dance styles have different rules and techniques. In some dances, dancers perform pre-planned steps. Other dances allow for **improvisation**. Some people become professional dancers. But many people dance for fun. Anyone who can move can dance.

Further Evidence

Look at the website below. Does it give any new evidence to support Chapter One?

Dance

abdocorelibrary.com/art-of-dance

Dance allows people to connect with their bodies.

CHAPTER 2

The Basics of Dance

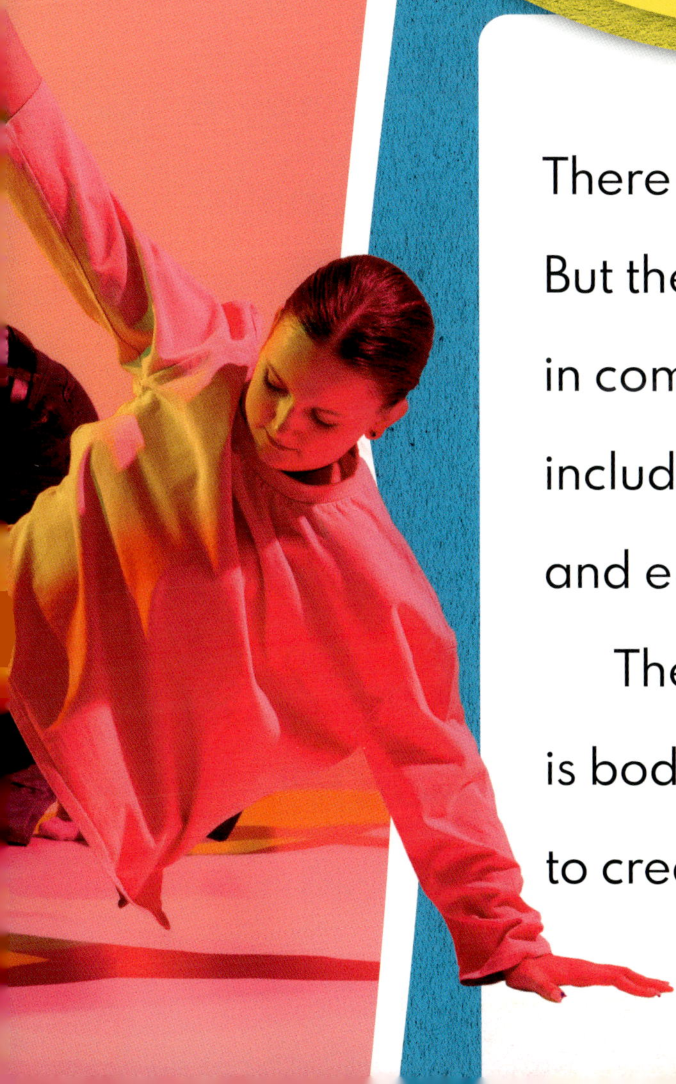

There are many types of dance. But they all have certain elements in common. These elements include body, action, space, time, and energy.

The first element of dance is body. Dancers use their bodies to create art. Next is action.

Action is the movement of a dancer's body. Dancers can jump, turn, or be still. Space is the area around a dancer. Dancers move in different directions.

Choreographers and dancers also work with time. The speed of the music and dance can be fast or slow. It can change throughout a dance. The final element of dance is energy. A dancer's movements may be slow and smooth or fast and sharp. Energy helps people express emotion.

Types of Dance

Ballet is a traditional performance dance from Europe. Some ballet performances tell a story. *The Nutcracker* and *Swan Lake* are

Only advanced ballerinas can dance on pointe. Pointe shoes are made of many layers of fabric, cardboard, and paper that are glued together.

famous story ballets. Other ballets focus on emotion instead of story. Some styles of ballet are very strict and traditional. Others use more modern techniques.

Bill "Bojangles" Robinson was a famous American tap dancer in the 1920s and 1930s.

Many American dance styles have African roots. Beginning in the 1600s and 1700s, enslaved African people were forced to work in poor conditions on large farms. Enslaved people from different cultures danced and played music to deal with their hard lives. Dancers often stomped and clapped to create rhythm. Over time, white performers copied the moves and began performing them in shows. This style eventually became known as jazz.

By the 1900s, jazz dancing had grown in popularity. Some jazz dancers added metal taps to the heels and toes of their shoes. This allowed them to make music with their feet. This style became known as tap dancing.

Tap and jazz dance became popular in movies and theater. In rhythm tap, dancers create their own music. Show tap dancers tap along with music and use more of their upper bodies. Jazz dancers use **syncopated** movements. They often move only one part of their bodies at a time.

In the late 1960s and early 1970s, the roots of jazz and tap inspired a new kind of dance. People in an area of New York City called the Bronx would dance together in the streets. Other people made music for the dancers. Hip-hop culture was born.

There are many dances that are part of hip-hop. These include breaking, popping,

Breaking

Breaking, or breakdancing, is a style of street dance. Breakers, called b-boys or b-girls, perform fancy footwork and **acrobatic** moves. These include top rocks, down rocks, freezes, and power moves. In 2024, breaking was an Olympic sport for the first time.

In 2023, artists celebrated the fiftieth anniversary of hip-hop.

and locking. But hip-hop is more than dance. Music, fashion, and graffiti are all parts of hip-hop culture.

Explore Online

Visit the website below. What new information about dance styles did you learn that wasn't in Chapter Two?

Glossary of Dance Terms

abdocorelibrary.com/art-of-dance

In 2017, professional dancer Misty Copeland performed as Kitri in the story ballet *Don Quixote*.

CHAPTER 3

Dance around the World

People around the world dance every day. Some people dance for work. Others dance for exercise or for fun. People can take classes at dance studios. Or they can take virtual lessons. People can watch performances in person or online.

On *So You Think You Can Dance,* dancers compete in themed dance challenges each week.

Dance is a big part of popular culture. Musicals often feature dancing. TV shows such as *Dancing with the Stars* and *So You Think You Can Dance* have made dance even more popular. Festivals and competitions highlight different dances from around the world.

Ginger Rogers and Fred Astaire were in ten films together from 1933 to 1949.

Famous Dancers

Many dancers have left their mark on history. Ginger Rogers and Fred Astaire are two famous dancers and actors. The pair performed ballroom and tap routines together.

Professional ballerina Misty Copeland did not begin taking formal dance lessons until she was 13. That is much later than most professionals start. But her teachers saw her potential. In 2015, Copeland became the first Black **principal dancer** at the American Ballet Theatre. She works to inspire young people and bring more diversity to ballet.

The Rockettes

The Rockettes are a world-famous American dance team. The team mainly performs at Radio City Music Hall in New York City. The Rockettes are known for their **synchronized** kick lines. To become a Rockette, dancers have to meet height requirements. They must also be skilled in ballet, tap, and jazz.

Les Twins performed at the Fusion Concept Festival World Final in 2022. Fusion Concept is an international hip-hop festival.

Laurent and Larry Bourgeois are the French hip-hop duo Les Twins. They rose to fame in street dances and hip-hop competitions. They were finalists on a French reality TV show before becoming dancers for famous singer Beyoncé.

Professional dancers may travel the world on concert tours.

Les Twins became famous worldwide when they won the competition TV show *World of Dance* in 2017. Since then, they have appeared in several movies and music videos.

People have been dancing since the dawn of time. They dance in different ways and for different reasons. But dance is an art form that brings people together. Today's dancers continue to inspire the dancers of tomorrow.

Primary Source

Debbie Allen is an award-winning dancer, choreographer, and actress. She founded a dance academy to give opportunities to people left out of traditional dance spaces. Allen said:

> All my life, I have known dance to **evoke** a certain energy, power, and self-confidence, which is why I think all people need to dance.

Source: Savannah M. Taylor. "Debbie Allen Speaks about Her Dance Academy's Partnership with the New Animated Series *Kiya and the Kimoja Heroes.*" *Ebony*, 10 Mar. 2023, ebony.com. Accessed 14 May 2024.

Point of View

What is the author's point of view on this topic? What is your point of view? Write a short essay about how they are similar and different.

Art Supplies

Short dress

Latin and Rhythm Ballroom

Dress shirt and dress pants

Open-toed shoes

Standard and Smooth Ballroom

Long dress

Closed-toed shoes

Hip-hop

Ballet

Tap

Glossary

acrobatic
involving skills such as jumping, tumbling, and balancing

choreographer
someone who creates dance routines

evoke
to call forth or bring up

improvisation
performing without a plan in place

prehistoric
having taken place before written history

principal dancer
the top dancer at a dance company

synchronized
performed at the same time

syncopated
stressed on beats that are not usually stressed

Online Resources

To learn more about dance, visit our free resource websites below.

Core Library CONNECTION
FREE! COMMON CORE MULTIMEDIA RESOURCES

Visit **abdocorelibrary.com** or scan this QR code for free Common Core resources for teachers and students, including vetted activities, multimedia, and booklinks, for deeper subject comprehension.

Booklinks NONFICTION NETWORK
FREE! ONLINE NONFICTION RESOURCES

Visit **abdobooklinks.com** or scan this QR code for free additional online weblinks for further learning. These links are routinely monitored and updated to provide the most current information available.

Learn More

Berrios, Frank. *The Story of Misty Copeland.* Rockridge, 2021.

Bode, Heather L. *Dance.* Abdo, 2024.

Murray, Julie. *Competitive Dance.* Abdo, 2023.

Index

About the Author

K. A. Hale has been a dancer almost her entire life. She studied ballet, pointe, and flamenco, and she was on her college's competitive ballroom team. She has also danced in musicals and show choir. Hale lives in Minnesota, where she writes, edits, and designs children's books full time.